MW00633359

When

TROLLEYS

RULED THE EARTH

A PHOTOGRAPHIC HISTORY OF STREETCARS,
CABLE CARS, AND CLASSIC TRAMS

by Mark Bussler

When Trolleys Ruled the Earth:
A Photographic History of Streetcars, Cable Cars, & Classic Trams

Written by Mark Bussler
Cover Design by Mark Bussler
Copyright © 2022 Inecom, LLC.
All Rights Reserved

No parts of this book may be reproduced or broadcast in any
way without written permission from Inecom, LLC.

www.CGRpublishing.com

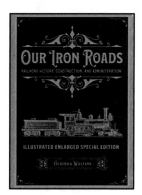

The Aeroplane Speaks: Illustrated Historical Guide to Airplanes

Antique Cars and Motor Vehicles: Illustrated Guide to Operation, Maintenance, and Repair

Our Iron Roads: Railroad History, Construction, and Administration

Boston Massachusetts, North Union Station

5

INTRODUCTION

My dad was always into trains, but it was all about the trolley for me. Trolleys ruled not just the rails but the roads as well. They pushed mere cars out of their way, bumped bystanders, and noisily scooted down city streets, delivering passengers where they needed to go. Trains were big and clumsy. Trolleys were like spaceships with wheels.

I vividly remember standing in downtown Pittsburgh with my dad around 1980. We watched a colorful, rounded trolley roll off the Smithfield Street Bridge (at least, that's how I remember it. I was very young.) The bridge and a Pittsburgh trolley are pictured on the next page.

Over the next few decades, Pittsburgh, like many other American cities, retired their aging fleet of trolleys, paved over the lines on the streets, and abolished cable cars in favor of busses and light rail service. There is no remaining evidence on the Smithfield Street Bridge that trolleys ever existed.

As I grew up, these vivid, futuristic trolleys faded from my imagination only to find themselves replaced with cars and video games. Many years later, in my professional life, I started to assemble a book project on commuter trains and stumbled across a color slide of one of those Pittsburgh trolleys. Immediately, I found myself transported back to 1980. Yes, the trolley was colorful and looked how I remember it, save for the noticeable wear and tear earned from years of service. It wasn't a dream. This thing was real.

Trolleys were awesome. What happened to them? Also, where did they come from?

Immediately, I remembered how much I liked trolleys. I changed the focus of my book project and assembled a collection of slides, negatives, and antique prints that spanned the life of the trolley from the horse-drawn tram to commuter rail service. All around the world, trolleys were an integral part of public transportation in major cities, small towns, and even rural areas! Trolleys took people to and from work and transported them to and fro, to clubs, restaurants, and arcades (while advertising cigarettes, booze, and lottery to unsuspecting bystanders. Oh, how I miss the '70s.)

And people loved them, as evidenced by the smiles on the color slide of one of San Francisco's famous cable cars pictures on page 68. Trolleys can be seen all over the place in 1900-era New York City, as pictured on pages 12 through 17. They ruled the road-rails in cities like Albany and Boston. Trolleys were fun. Trolleys were functional. Riding a trolley was way better than stepping in piles of horse poo or hailing a car from a ride-share app.

Take a trip back down memory lane with me and enjoy a delightful and nostalgic look at the days when trolleys ruled the earth. I ride my bike over the Smithfield Street Bridge frequently and always think about that colorful trolley. You are remembered, friend!

- Mark Bussler

Grattan Bridge Dublin, & River Liffey

A 5 - The Escolta. The principal business street of Manila, Philippines.

Street Cars, Strong City, Kans.

11

Cedar St.   Mercantile Safe Deposit Co.   Broadway   Equitable Building   Mercantile Tr. Co.   Am. Surety Co.

EQUITABLE LIFE ASSURANCE SOCIETY, 120 B'way; Nassau St., Cedar to Pine Sts.; founded 1859 by H. B. Hyde; re-organized 1905, Grover Cleveland, Morgan J. O'Brien and Geo. Westinghouse trustees of majority stock owned by Thos. F. Ryan; one of largest life-insurance companies; policies in force, $1,500,000,000; surplus, $65,000,000; assets, $430,000,000. Paul Morton, Pres.

Singer Tower   Iron Worker 540 ft. above street   Broadway   Dun Bldg.   P. O.   St. Paul Bldg.   Park Row Bldg., 382 ft.

BROADWAY, looking north from Singer Tower. Photo by Brown Bros. from height of 540 ft., showing main thoroughfare of New York, congested East Side with East River beyond. Park Row Bldg. with twin cupolas, long the highest in the world, St. Paul Bldg., 317 ft., and massive Federal Bldg., appear dwarfed from this elevation, and the people in the streets are mere specks.

COPYRIGHT 1907
BY MOSES KING.

R.W. Rummel

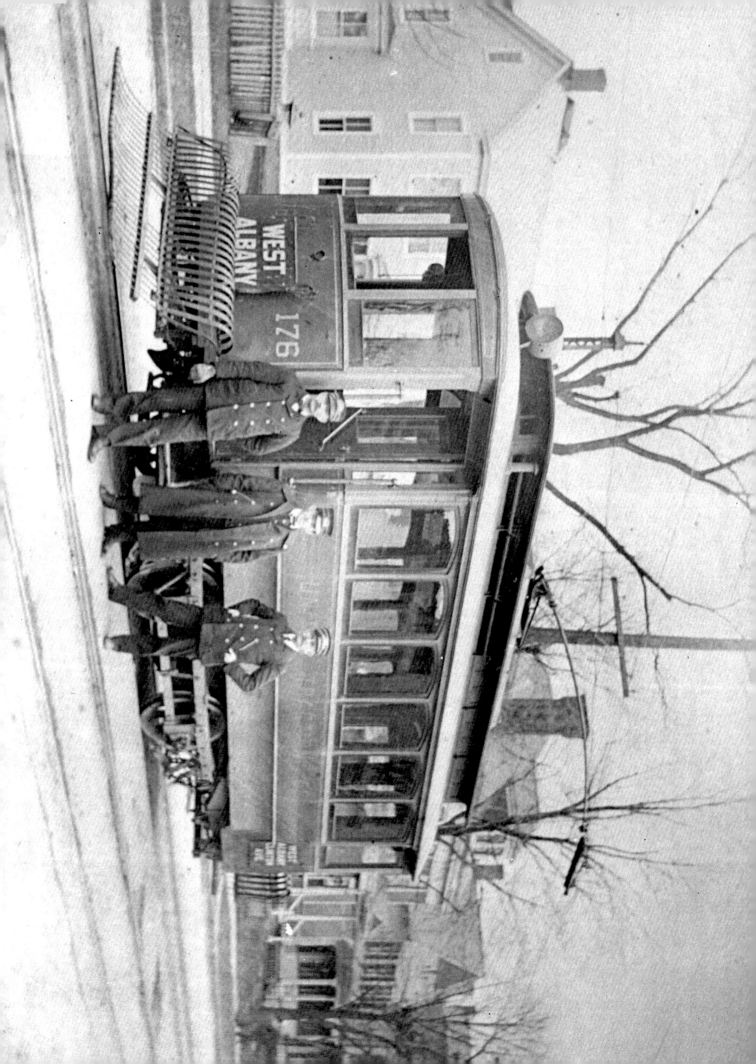

Superior St. Viaduct, Cleveland, Ohio.

Dear Edgar - Rec'd your postal:
will try & write you a letter soon.
I spent a great day in Cleveland
today. will explain in letter -
Hubert -

1195   BUFFALO N.Y. & DRESDEN GERMANY

Canal Street by night. New Orleans, Louisiana.

Yokohama, Japan.

COMPLETE CATALOG OF BOOKS AT CGRPUBLISHING.COM

Historic Cathedrals of England: A Classic Illustrated Guide

1901 Buffalo World's Fair: The Pan-American Exposition in Photographs

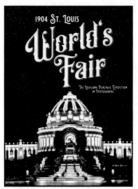

1904 St. Louis World's Fair: The Louisiana Purchase Exposition in Photographs

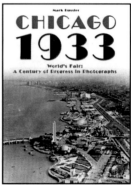

Chicago 1933 World's Fair: A Century of Progress in Photographs

1915 San Francisco World's Fair in Color: Grandeur of the Panama-Pacific...

The American Railway: The Trains, Railroads, and People Who Ran the Rails

The Aeroplane Speaks: Illustrated Historical Guide to Airplanes

The World's Fair of 1893 Ultra Massive Photographic Adventure Vol. 1

The White City of Color: 1893 World's Fair

The Classic Guide to Still Life and Figure Drawing

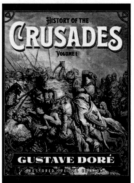

History of the Crusades: Gustave Doré Retro Restored Edition

History in the Age of Vikings: Volumes 1-3

101 Cars on Stamps: The Art of Motor Vehicles on Postage Stamps

The Complete Ford Model T Guide: Enlarged Illustrated Special Edition

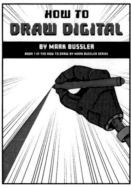

How To Draw Digital by Mark Bussler

Best of Gustave Doré Volume 1: Illustrations from History's Most Versatile...

Ultra Massive Video Game Console
Guide Volume 1

Dante's Inferno:
Retro Hell-Bound Edition

The Classic Guide to Sketching and
Drawing with Pencils

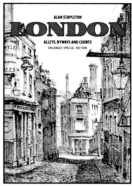

London Alleys, Byways, and Courts:
Enlarged Special Edition

Antique Cars and Motor Vehicles:
Illustrated Guide to Operation...

Chicago's White City Cookbook

The Clock Book: A Detailed Illustrated
Collection of Classic Clocks

The Complete Book of Birds: Illustrated
Enlarged Special Edition

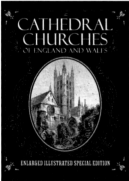

The Cathedral Churches of England and
Wales: Enlarged Illustrated Special Ed.

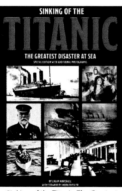

Sinking of the Titanic: The Greatest
Disaster at Sea

Gustave Doré's London: A Pilgrimage:
Retro Restored Special Edition

Milton's Paradise Lost: Gustave Doré
Retro Restored Edition

The Art of World War 1

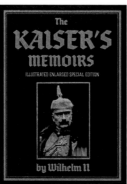

The Kaiser's Memoirs: Illustrated
Enlarged Special Edition

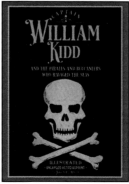

Captain William Kidd and the Pirates
and Buccaneers Who Ravaged the Seas

The Complete Butterfly Book: Enlarged
Illustrated Special Edition

TURBO VOLCANO
turbovolcano.com

ABOUT WRITER / ARTIST
MARK BUSSLER

Writer, artist, musician, and publisher Mark Bussler has written more than 100 books and designed over 300 covers for CGR Publishing. Bussler is a professional artist and commercial designer who works in digital and physical media. He created and continues to develop the *Robot Kitten Factory* series, *Retromegatrex*, *How to Draw Inspired by Classic Illustrations*, and other graphic novels and instructional guides. Additionally, he writes history books and photographic history collections such as *1904 St. Louis World's Fair: The Louisiana Purchase Exposition in Photographs*. Bussler previously produced and directed films such as *Westinghouse, Expo: Magic of the White City*, and the *Classic Game Room* series. He is the founder and president of CGR Publishing, and founder of the industrial synthesizer laser-disco band, *Turbo Volcano* and the ambient synth group, *Seatropica*. Bussler produces and hosts the weekly CGR Podcast featuring Turbo Volcano.

SELECT PUBLISHED WORKS

BOOKS:
Best of Gustave Doré Volume 1: Illustrations from History's Most Versatile Artist
Best of Gustave Doré Volume 2: Illustrations from History's Most Versatile Artist
Robot Kitten Factory #1
Robot Kitten Factory #2
Robot Kitten Factory #3 (2022)
How To Draw Digital by Mark Bussler
How To Draw Pandas by Mark Bussler
1915 San Francisco World's Fair in Color: Grandeur of the Panama-Pacific Exposition
1939 New York World's Fair: The World of Tomorrow in Photographs Volume 1
1939 New York World's Fair: The World of Tomorrow in Photographs Volume 2
1904 St. Louis World's Fair: The Louisiana Purchase Exposition in Photographs
1901 Buffalo World's Fair: The Pan-American World's Fair in Photographs
Magnum Skywolf #1
Ultra Massive Video Game Console Guide 1
Ultra Massive Video Game Console Guide 2
Ultra Massive Video Game Console Guide 3
Ultra Massive Sega Genesis Guide
All Hail the Vectrex: Ultimate Collector's Review Guide
Chicago 1933 World's Fair: A Century of Progress in Photographs
Ethel the Cyborg Ninja #1
Ethel the Cyborg Ninja #2
Ethel the Cyborg Ninja #3 (2022)
The World's Fair of 1893 Ultra Massive Photographic Adventure Volume 1
The World's Fair of 1893 Ultra Massive Photographic Adventure Volume 2
The World's Fair of 1893 Ultra Massive Photographic Adventure Volume 3
The White City of Color: 1893 World's Fair
Retromegatrex 1: The Lost Art of Mark Bussler 1995-2017
Retromegatrex 2: The Art of Mark Bussler 2018-2022
Lord Karnage 1.5 Special Edition
Historic Cathedrals of England: A Classic Illustrated Guide (Restoration)
Classic Cars and Automobile Engineering: Volume 1 (Restoration)
Classic Cars and Automobile Engineering: Volume 2 (Restoration)
Classic Cars and Automobile Engineering: Volume 3 (Restoration)
Classic Cars and Automobile Engineering: Volume 4 (Restoration)
Classic Cars and Automobile Engineering: Volume 5 (Restoration)
Old Timey Pictures with Silly Captions Volume 1
Old Timey Pictures with Silly Captions Volume 2
Old Timey Pictures with Silly Captions Volume 3
The Art of Ferdinand Von Reznicek Volume 1
How to Draw Womens' Eyes: Inspired by Classic Illustrations Volume 1
When Trolleys Ruled the Earth: A Photographic History of Streetcars, Cable Cars, & Classic Trams
When Our Antique Car was Brand New and Lost Family Photographs of Classic Automobiles
How to Draw Mens' Eyes: Inspired by Classic Illustrations Volume 2 (2022)

MUSIC:
Turbo Volcano: Future Year 1982
Turbo Volcano: Supernova Robot Dungeon
Seatropica: Abyss

CGR PODCAST

featuring

TURBO VOLCANO

WEEKLY PODCAST ON ALL MAJOR PLATFORMS

CGRpublishing.com
TurboVolcano.com